350
Questions

LDS COUPLES SHOULD ASK
BEFORE MARRIAGE

Other books by Shannon L. Alder

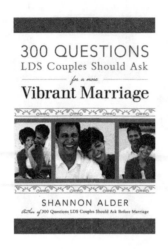

300 Questions LDS Couples Should Ask for a More Vibrant Marriage

300 Questions to Ask Your Parents before It's Too Late

350
Questions

**LDS COUPLES SHOULD ASK
BEFORE MARRIAGE**

SHANNON L. ALDER

CFI
An imprint of Cedar Fort, Inc.
Springville, Utah

This is not an official publication of The Church of Jesus Christ of Latter-day Saints. The opinions and views expressed herein belong solely to the author and do not necessarily represent the opinions or views of Cedar Fort, Inc. Permission for the use of sources, graphics, and photos is also solely the responsibility of the author.

ISBN 13: 978-1-4621-2179-3

Published by CFI, an imprint of Cedar Fort, Inc.
2373 W. 700 S., Springville, UT, 84663
Distributed by Cedar Fort, Inc., www.cedarfort.com

Library of Congress Control Number: 2017958784

Cover design by Angela Olsen and Katie Payne
Cover design © 2018 Cedar Fort, Inc.
Typeset by Sydnee Hyer

Printed in the United States of America

10   9   8   7   6   5   4   3   2   1

Printed on acid-free paper

Affectionately dedicated to my loving husband, Jim,
who continues to support all of my writing endeavors.
You are my true eternal companion!

Table of Questions

"Courtship is a wonderful period. It should be a sacred one. That is the time in which you choose your mate."

President David O. McKay
(*True to the Faith*, Bookcraft, 1966, 317.)

Introduction

Research shows that poor communication is the leading reason for divorce. However, poor communication doesn't begin in marriage; it starts well before, in the dating stage of the relationship. The way we communicate in dating and courtship is key to building a solid marital relationship. Elder Marvin J. Ashton of the Quorum of the Twelve Apostles said: "If we would know true love and understanding one for another, we must realize that communication is more than a sharing of words. It is the wise sharing of emotions, feelings, and concerns. It is the sharing of oneself totally (Marvin J. Ashton, "Family Communications," *Ensign*, May 1976, 52). To share themselves totally, a couple must ask and answer questions that will help them decide if they are compatible for such an important commitment as marriage. For example, Do you really know this person? Have you asked all the questions you need to ask to make sure the two of you are compatible? Do you share similar thoughts and dreams? Does he or she live by the principles of the gospel? Does he or she have a strong testimony? Does he magnify his priesthood and live righteously? Will she or he make a good mother or father? These are just a few of the many questions I have compiled in this book for you.

We should weigh a potential spouse's character and our ability to create a good relationship with that person, but we should not forget to consider past and present family relationships. We each bring to our relationships an "emotional genealogy" that is created by all the relationships we had as we grew up. How did our families handle money? What were their values concerning work? Did they spend a lot of time focusing on the family or were they individuals living in the same house? What about the strength of his or her testimony? Role expectations? Financial issues? President David O. McKay taught, "In choosing a companion, it is necessary to study the disposition, the inheritance, and training of the one with whom you are contemplating making life's journey" (*Gospel Ideals*, 1953, 459).

Many couples don't ask these important questions; they believe that love is enough and leave everything else to fate. However, as the book of James reminds us, it is not enough just to believe something; we must act upon it (James 1:25, 2:15–18, 3:13). We shouldn't leave things to fate. Sometimes, we are given false expectations by movies, plays, and fiction that promote the idea that there is a "one and only" somewhere out there whom we are intended to marry. Many people believe that finding a mate means locking eyes with them across a crowded room and instantly falling in love, and then they live happily ever after. No matter how romantic this idea is, it is not supported by prophetic counsel. President Spencer W. Kimball taught us that "soul mates" are a fiction and an illusion; and while every young man and young woman will seek with all diligence and prayerfulness to find a mate with whom life can be beautiful, it is certain that almost any good man and any good woman can have happiness and a successful marriage if both are willing to pay the price (*Marriage and Divorce*, 1976, 16). He further states, "While I am sure some young couples have some special guidance in getting together, I do not believe in predestined love. If you desire the inspiration of the Lord in this crucial decision, you must live the standards of the Church, and you must pray constantly for the wisdom to recognize those qualities upon which a successful union may be based. You must do the choosing, rather than to seek for some one-and-only so-called soul mate, chosen for you by someone else and waiting for you. You are to do the choosing. You must be wise beyond your years and humbly prayerful unless you choose amiss" (*Eternal Love*, Salt Lake City: Deseret Book Co., 1973, 11). Therefore, arming yourself with the questions to be asked when seeking your eternal companion will help you weed out those who are not compatible and will only bring sadness to your life.

This book is not a list of questions that suggest perfection is required. There are no right and wrong answers. But these questions are to be answered from the heart. No question can be asked that you are not willing to answer yourself. The prophet counsels us to be selective when choosing a mate. We should choose someone who is most compatible and will help us achieve righteous objectives. Even though a couple may be very busy with wedding preparations, it is critical that they make time to prepare for their lifetime together by exploring their relationship in more depth. Communication, along with a willingness to grow closer together, is the key to a successful marriage.

"Don't let this choice [of a marriage partner] ever be made except with earnest, searching, prayerful consideration, confiding in parents, [and] in faithful, mature, trustworthy friends."

Elder Richard L. Evans (1906–71)
of the Quorum of the Twelve Apostles

("This You Can Count On," *Improvement Era,* **Dec. 1969, 73.)**

"You use every faculty, you get all the judgment that you can centered on the problem, you make up your own mind, and then, to be sure that you don't err, you counsel with the Lord. You talk it over. You say, "This is what I think; what do you think?" And if you get the calm, sweet surety that comes only from the Holy Spirit, you know you've reached the right conclusion; but if there's anxiety and uncertainty in your heart, then you'd better start over, because the Lord's hand is not in it, and you're not getting the ratifying seal that, as a member of the Church who has the gift of the Holy Ghost, you are entitled to receive."

Elder Bruce R. McConkie

("Agency or Inspiration—Which?" Speeches of the Year,
BYU Devotional Addresses, 1972–73, 115–16.)

Spiritual Questions

1. Do you have a strong testimony of the Church? What areas of your testimony are weak and will cause problems later on in your relationship? What areas do you expect to be strong when you have children?

_____

_____

_____

_____

_____

_____

2. Are you able to hold a temple recommend?

_____

3. Do you live the teachings of the gospel? Attend all meetings, pay tithing and live righteously?

_____

_____

_____

4. Do you each accept the patriarchal order? Is he the type of priesthood holder that you really trust? Are you willing to counsel together in love, but if necessary, abide by his counsel in righteousness and follow him in a spirit of genuine willingness?

_____

_____

_____

_____

5. Can you call upon him in full faith and confidence to give you a special blessing when you desire?

_____

_____

6. Do you pray together? Read scriptures together?

_____

7. Have you read your patriarchal blessing together? Do you believe that he or she can help you achieve these blessings?

_____

_____

_____

8. Do you fully obey your priesthood leaders in all righteousness? Is this someone you spiritually admire?

_____

_____

_____

9. Does she inspire you to be a righteous priesthood leader in your home?

_____

_____

_____

10. What will your destiny together be? Your potential destiny is that of god and goddess. If each of you continues to progress as you are now, is godhood likely? Will your prospective mate help you to achieve that great destiny?

_____

_____

_____

_____

_____

_____

11. Do you both accept the law of perfection and the principle of eternal progression? Does each of you see the other as becoming perfect?

_____

_____

_____

_____

_____

_____

12. Do you live the Words of Wisdom? Is each of you happy with the other's approach to health? Does one have habits or tendencies that concern the other (e.g., smoking, excessive dieting, poor diet)?

_____

_____

_____

_____

_____

_____

_____

13. Has he served a mission? If not, would he be resentful or regretful later on if he didn't serve one? Are you keeping him from going on a mission because of your insecurities or selfishness?

_____

_____

_____

_____

14. What will be the role of faith in your marriage?

_____

_____

_____

_____

15. What are you not prepared to sacrifice when you get married? Do you feel at ease kneeling in prayer to ask for guidance on specific issues that effect you as a couple?

_____

_____

_____

_____

_____

16. What is your definition of a "celestial marriage"?

_____

_____

_____

_____

_____

_____

17. Is the destiny of godhood one that both of you have accepted and one that you want to help each other achieve?

_____

_____

_____

_____

_____

18. Do you observe the Sabbath? Is it important that your children observe it?

_____

_____

19. What place does the Mormon religion have in your life? Will it always be first or is something else more important?

_____

_____

_____

_____

_____

20. What would cause you not to attend church?

_____

_____

_____

_____

_____

21. If I chose to become inactive or leave the Church, would we divorce?

_____

_____

_____

_____

22. Have you done anything wrong that you would need to see a bishop to get resolved?

_____

_____

_____

23. What do you believe is the purpose of life?

_____

_____

_____

_____

_____

_____

_____

24. How do you feel about fast offerings and giving to local charities?

_____

_____

_____

25. Do you believe that the Church of Jesus Christ is the only true religion?

_____

_____

26. If you had to describe your spiritual life in 10 words, what would they be and why?

_____

_____

_____

_____

_____

_____

_____

_____

_____

_____

27. How forgiving are you? Who in your life have you not forgiven?

_____

_____

_____

_____

_____

28. How often do you expect to visit the temple? Monthly? Yearly?

_____

_____

_____

29. How important is it that your children serve missions?

_____

_____

_____

_____

30. Do you both keep the Sabbath Day holy? Is there something he/she does on the Sabbath that you don't agree with?

_____

_____

_____

_____

31. Do you hold all your callings or turn some down when a calling is extended to you?

_____

_____

_____

_____

32. Have you prayed to see if this person is the correct person for you? What was your answer?

_____

_____

_____

_____

_____

_____

_____

33. Once an issue has been carefully and prayerfully considered, do you accept the final decision willingly—or rebel against it?

_____

_____

_____

34. Is he honoring his priesthood so that he will be able to bless your children in times of illness or other needs?

_____

_____

_____

35. Will you have weekly family home evenings?

_____

_____

36. What are your views on polygamy? If this ordinance were allowed would you consider taking another wife?

_____

_____

_____

_____

37. Do you watch R-rated movies? What rating of movie will you allow your future children to see?

_____

_____

38. Do you listen to the still, small voice and make life decisions based on it? How do you balance inspiration and research?

_____

_____

_____

_____

_____

39. Do you buy things on Sunday? Do you plan for your future children to buy on Sunday also?

_____

_____

_____

"The successful marriage depends in large measure upon the preparation made in approaching it ... One cannot pick the ripe, rich, luscious fruit from a tree that was never planted, nurtured, nor pruned."

President Spencer W. Kimball

(*The Miracle of Forgiveness*, Salt Lake City: Bookcraft, 1969, 242.)

"I suggest that you not ignore many possible candidates who are still developing these attributes, seeking the one who is perfected in them. You will likely not find that perfect person, and if you did, there would certainly be no interest in you. These attributes are best polished together as husband and wife."

Elder Richard G. Scott of the Quorum of the Twelve Apostles

(*Ensign*, May 1999, 26.)

Family Questions

1. How does each of you feel about the other being a parent of your children? Will you be the type of mother or father that you really wish for your children? And will you want your children to be like him or her? (They probably will be.)

_____

_____

_____

_____

_____

_____

2. Are you each now, or are you becoming, the type of individuals that you would be happy to have your children become?

_____

_____

_____

_____

_____

3. Have you discussed your goals for parenthood? And do you both agree upon and accept the gospel plan of bringing children into your home?

_____

_____

_____

_____

_____

4. How many children do each of you want to have, and when do you plan to start a family?

_____

_____

5. How far apart do you want kids?

_____

6. Accidental pregnancy, what do we do?

_____

_____

_____

7. Do you trust her to help your children learn to be obedient to your righteous direction by being a good role model for them?

_____

_____

_____

_____

_____

8. Do either of you feel that you need to complete college before getting married and starting a family? If you had a family before those dreams became realized, would you be resentful?

_____

_____

_____

_____

9. Are you prepared to marry the family of your prospective mate? While you may think that you only marry one person, in a real sense, you marry into a whole family. The parents of your mate become the grandparents of your children. Do you each feel good about that—and the influence they will have on your children?

_____

_____

_____

_____

10. If he or she is unable to have children, how will that affect your relationship? Are you open to adoption?

_____

_____

_____

_____

11. Would you be willing to seek medical treatment if we couldn't have kids naturally?

_____

_____

_____

_____

12. What place does his or her family play in your life? How often do you visit or socialize together? If you have out-of-town relatives, will you ask them to visit you for extended periods? How often? For what length of time?

_____

_____

_____

_____

_____

_____

_____

13. If you were to have children, what kind of relationship do you hope your parents will have with their grandchildren? How much time will they spend together?

_____

_____

_____

_____

14. How will having a child change the way you live now? Will you want to or be able to take time off from work, or work a reduced schedule? For how long?

_____

_____

_____

_____

_____

_____

15. Would you want someone to stay home with the kids or use daycare?

_____

_____

_____

16. If your primary language is not English, what language will you raise your children learning?

_____

_____

17. How important is having children to each of you?

_____

_____

_____

_____

18. How is your relationship with your mother or siblings?

_____

_____

_____

19. How did your family resolve conflicts when you were growing up? Do you approve or disapprove of that method? what will you change or not change to resolve conflicts in your future family?

_____

_____

_____

_____

20. What did you admire about the way your mother and father treated each other?

_____

_____

_____

_____

21. What does his or her family do that annoys you?

_____

_____

_____

_____

_____

_____

22. Do you think you will have problems with your family during the holidays? What values do you want to bring from your family into your marriage?

_____

_____

_____

_____

_____

_____

23. Do you believe in using birth control? Or letting the Lord provide?

_____

_____

_____

_____

_____

24. What is your interpretation of our Church's opinion on contraception?

_____

_____

_____

_____

_____

25. Does each of you expect your children to be married in the temple? How will you live so your expectation happens?

_____

_____

_____

_____

_____

26. If he/she were once married, how would you feel if his/her ex-spouse rang him/her constantly to discuss children, child support, bills or just to talk casually?

_____

_____

_____

_____

_____

27. Would you feel uncomfortable if he/she went over to his/her ex's house to pick up the children or to discuss visitation or another topic without you present?

_____

_____

_____

28. What type of discipline would you implement, to correct your child or teenager's behavior? Do you believe in spanking, the "time-out chair" or something else?

_____

_____

_____

_____

29. Do you believe it's okay to discipline your child in public?

_____

30. At what age do you think your kids should be allowed to single date or group date?

_____

31. How will we handle parental decisions if we disagree?

_____

_____

_____

_____

_____

32. Who comes first, your spouse or your children?

_____

_____

_____

33. Do you believe in the youth program of the Church? Do you want your children to be actively involved in young women and boy scouts?

_____

_____

34. Is it important for you to live by your mother, if you have children?

_____

35. Is there a certain family name that you are adamant about giving to your children?

_____

36. Are you planning to have anyone in your family live with you in the future? Do you both agree to this?

_____

_____

37. Our parents are getting old, what do we do?

_____

_____

_____

_____

38. Do you believe in abortion in your family? What if you knew in advance that the baby wouldn't live long after birth, or would have a difficult life?

_____

_____

_____

39. If you have children from a previous relationship, what is your relationship with those children now?

_____

_____

_____

_____

40. What is the best method of raising children?

_____

_____

_____

_____

_____

_____

41. Do you believe in public schools for your children?

_____

_____

42. Do you believe in home-schooling your children? If so, by whom?

_____

_____

43. What type of relationship should your children have with non-Mormon classmates and friends?

_____

_____

_____

44. Would you send your children to visit their extended family, if they lived in another state or country?

_____

_____

45. If there are members of your family that are not Mormon (i.e., that are of a different culture, race or religion), what type of relationship do you want to have with them? What if these family members don't have the same standards or values as yours?

_____

_____

_____

_____

_____

_____

_____

46. Would it bother you if his or her family stopped by your home often to visit? Do you get along with his or her family?

_____

_____

_____

_____

47. Do you expect all of your children to serve missions for the Church?

_____

48. If your significant other was married before, would you feel uncomfortable if he/she maintained a close friendship with his/her ex-spouse or ex-in-laws?

_____

_____

_____

49. What are your views on homosexuality? If your son or daughter expressed to you that they had these feelings, what counsel would you give them?

_____

_____

_____

_____

_____

_____

"Choose a companion of your own faith. You are much more likely to be happy. Choose a companion you can always honor, you can always respect, one who will complement you in your own life, one to whom you can give your entire heart, your entire love, your entire allegiance, your entire loyalty."

President Gordon B. Hinckley

(*Ensign*, Feb. 1999, 2.)

Finance Questions

1. Does he or she seek your opinion on issues involving finance, including where to live or large items to buy (house, car, etc.)? Or, does he/she take care of these big decisions without you?

_____

_____

_____

_____

2. What have you done financially to prepare for marriage? Are you in debt? Are you good with money or spend it without any thought for the future?

_____

_____

_____

3. Is there something you are saving for?

_____

_____

_____

4. How much money do you earn together? Now? In one year? In five years? Ten? Who is responsible for which portion? Now? In one year? Five? Ten?

---

5. What is your ultimate financial goal regarding annual income, and when do you anticipate achieving it? By what means, and through what efforts? Will there be enough to pay tithing?

---

6. How much time does each of you spend at work? If one of you doesn't want to work outside the home, under what circumstances, if any, would that be okay?

---

7. Fired/laid off from job, what do we do?

_____

_____

_____

_____

8. Financial crunch (car problems, medical bills, leaking water pipes, etc.), what do we do?

_____

_____

_____

_____

9. How much do you spend monthly and annually, and in each category (rent, clothing, food, electricity, car, school loan)? How much do you want to be able to spend? Now? In one year? Five? Ten?

_____

_____

_____

_____

10. Is my debt your debt? Would you be willing to bail me out?

_____

_____

_____

_____

11. Do you trust me with money?

_____

12. How ambitious are you? Are you comfortable with the other's level of ambition? Do you have high expectations that are unrealistic and don't match his/her desires? Do you expect him/her to have a certain type of job and salary within a certain time frame?

_____

_____

_____

13. If you became very ill or lost your job and was unable to work, would he/she be able to take care of your financial needs? Do you have enough saved just in case something like that were to happen?

_____

_____

_____

_____

14. Does it matter to you who earns most of the money?

_____

_____

15. Are you a saver or spender when it comes to money? Do you want to have a budget?

_____

_____

16. Should you have a joint checking account, or separate accounts, or both?

_____

17. Who is going to be responsible for making sure that bills are paid on time?

_____

18. Do you prefer to pay by cash, credit card or by checks? Is there one way you want your family to pay for routine things consistently?

_____

_____

19. Are you going to rent or buy?

_____

_____

20. How do you see us 10 years from now?

_____

_____

_____

_____

_____

21. When do you expect to buy a new house? For how much? Do you have money saved for a down payment?

_____

_____

_____

22. Are you prepared in case of a family emergency? Do you have a one-year food supply in case of such an event?

_____

_____

_____

23. What do you think is a reasonable amount to spend on clothes and personal items each month? What about entertainment?

_____

_____

_____

24. Would you ever take financial help if you lost your job? Either from the Church or welfare? Why or why not?

_____

_____

_____

_____

25. What do you know about investments in property or stocks and bonds?

_____

_____

_____

_____

26. What do you know about mortgages, interest rates, and applying for loans?

_____

_____

_____

_____

27. How often do you use your credit cards? Have you ever been denied a credit card or maxed them out?

_____

_____

28. What is your credit rating?

_____

29. Should your children pay for their own college?

_____

30. Should your children pay for their own mission?

_____

31. How much do you owe in student loans?

_____

32. How do you save your money?

_____

_____

_____

33. What is your definition of "wealth"?

_____

_____

_____

_____

_____

34. How do you think that your use of money will change after marriage?

_____

_____

_____

_____

35. Do you support the idea of taking loans to buy a new home?

_____

36. What are you expecting from your spouse financially?

_____

_____

_____

37. Do you think is okay to borrow money from family and friends? What is a reasonable amount of time that should be repaid?

_____

_____

_____

38. If you have children from a previous marriage, do you feel it is acceptable to give those children more money than what you currently pay in child support?

_____

_____

_____

39. Are you currently paying child support? On time?

_____

_____

40. How would you feel about not leaving the state because your significant other has children within the state whom he or she has joint custody of, and must see weekly?

_____

_____

41. Do you feel your children should buy their own cars and have jobs in high school to pay for them?

_____

_____

_____

42. Do you travel often? How important is this to you? What if you can't do this financially anymore?

_____

_____

_____

43. Do you plan to pay tithing based on your net income or gross income?

_____

_____

44. How attached are you to your pets? Would you be willing to spend $100, $1,000 or more to save their lives?

_____

_____

_____

45. How important is money to you? If you lived poorly most of your life, would your feelings for one another be any less than they are now?

_____

_____

_____

_____

_____

_____

_____

"Soul mates are a fiction and an illusion; and while every young man and young woman will seek with all diligence and prayerfulness to find a mate with whom life can be beautiful, it is certain that almost any good man and any good woman can have happiness and a successful marriage if both are willing to pay the price."

President Spencer W. Kimball

(*Marriage and Divorce*, Brigham Young University
devotional, September 7, 1976, 16 [See speeches.edu.byu].)

Expectations
Questions

1. What relationship do you expect your spouse to have with your children and their parent?

_____

_____

_____

_____

_____

_____

_____

2. Do you support the idea of a working wife?

_____

_____

_____

3. Do you support the idea of utilizing baby-sitters and maids?

_____

_____

4. What role expectations do you have? Who is responsible for keeping the house and yard cared for and organized? Who is responsible for cooking and bills?

_____

_____

_____

_____

5. Are you different in your need for cleanliness and organization? Is one or both of you neat? Messy? A "pack rat?" An organizational wizard? Could you live with a slob?

_____

_____

_____

_____

6. What are the most important characteristics of a mate that are socially and spiritually appealing to you? Do you possess all of them?

_____

_____

_____

_____

_____

_____

_____

7. What do you, as a couple, want out of life?

_____

_____

_____

_____

_____

8. Do you consider going to the movies and having a vacation every year a necessity or a luxury?

_____

_____

9. Do you believe that you should be doing everything together? Can you each pursue your own interests?

_____

_____

10. What do you consider "quality time" with him or her?

_____

_____

_____

_____

11. Some professions are very demanding. If he or she plans to be a doctor or other occupation that requires a lot of time for training, how will you cope with his or her absence?

_____

_____

_____

12. If he or she is in the military, do you respect that profession? How will you cope if he/she is called abroad?

_____

_____

_____

13. What are your expectations of marriage? Do you expect perfection? A fairy tale? A soap opera? Are you realistic?

_____

_____

_____

_____

_____

14. What are three things that you want to accomplish in the near future?

_____

_____

_____

_____

_____

_____

_____

15. What are your expectations in life? Can you list your long-term and your short-term goals for yourself and for your family?

_____

_____

_____

_____

_____

_____

_____

_____

_____

16. What do you expect the role of a husband to be like?

_____

_____

_____

_____

_____

17. What do you expect the role of a wife to be like?

_____

_____

_____

_____

_____

18. If your husband was extended the calling of bishop, what do you expect in terms of quality time given to the family? (Keep in mind that this is a very time-consuming job.)

_____

_____

_____

_____

19. What do you expect the relationship between your spouse and your family to be like?

_____

_____

_____

_____

_____

20. What are you expecting from your spouse when your friends come to your home?

_____

_____

_____

_____

21. How do you expect to spend your vacations?

_____

_____

_____

_____

22. How do you think your spouse should spend vacations? Are separate vacations okay with you?

_____

_____

_____

23. Once married, do you expect your spouse to express romantic feelings daily?

_____

_____

24. Once married, do you expect your spouse to express affection in public?

_____

_____

25. If someone has wronged you, how do you want them to apologize to you?

_____

_____

_____

_____

26. Do you plan to care for your parents when they are elderly? If "yes": even if it means they have to live with you?

_____

_____

_____

27. Are household duties dependent on the gender of each person?

_____

_____

_____

28. Do you expect time alone? How often? How would you feel if he/she had a night out with his/her friends once a week? Once a month?

_____

_____

_____

_____

_____

29. Do you think seriously about the future, or do you just take it for granted that all will be fine?

_____

_____

30. Do you dream of a specific place you want to live? Are you willing to compromise?

_____

_____

_____

31. Do you expect your kids to go to BYU colleges or is a non-LDS college okay? What if they were given a scholarship to a non-Mormon school?

_____

_____

_____

_____

32. Are you sentimental? How important is it to you if they forget birthdays or certain holidays? Do you expect lavish gifts and cards?

_____

_____

_____

_____

_____

33. What are you expecting of your spouse, in terms of religion?

_____

_____

_____

_____

_____

_____

34. Do you expect a new home or certain income by a certain age or number of years after marriage?

_____

_____

_____

35. Do you think you will have problems with your families during the holidays?

_____

_____

_____

36. Are there some things that you and I are NOT prepared to give up in the marriage?

_____

_____

_____

_____

37. Do you expect to go on a couple's mission? How important is it to you?

_____

_____

_____

_____

38. Do you expect intimacy often? Do you feel you have the right to demand it?

_____

_____

_____

_____

_____

"If the choice is between reforming other Church members [including fiancés, spouses, and children] or ourselves, is there really any question about where we should begin? The key is to have our eyes wide open to our own faults and partially closed to the faults of others-not the other way around! The imperfections of others never release us from the need to work on our own shortcomings."

Elder Neal A. Maxwell of the Quorum of the Twelve Apostles

("A Brother Offended," *Ensign*, May 1982, 39.)

Your Relationship
Questions

1. Do you help one another to have more self-esteem, or do you tend to find fault with each other? Are his/her needs as important to you as your own?

_____

_____

_____

_____

_____

2. How do you each treat your own parents? Do you respect them as individuals and respect their position and authority? (It is likely that you will treat each other the same way you each treat own family.)

_____

_____

_____

_____

3. Do your friends use foul language? Does your family use foul language?

_____

4. Do you use foul language at home? In public? With your family?

_____

5. Are you satisfied with the quality and quantity of friends you currently have? Would you like to be more involved socially? Are you overwhelmed socially, and do you need to cut back on such commitments?

_____

_____

_____

_____

6. What are your partner's needs for cultivating or maintaining friendships outside of your relationship? Is it easy for you to support those needs, or do they bother you in any way?

_____

_____

_____

_____

7. Sometimes we lose perspective and the best source for opinions is our friends and family. What does your friends and family think of him or her?

_____

_____

_____

8. Do you feel the need to maintain relationships with your past boy-friends/girlfriends? Why or why not?

_____

_____

_____

9. Would you expect him or her not to spend any time alone with friends that are of the opposite sex?

_____

_____

_____

10. Do you anticipate maintaining your single lifestyle after you are married? That is: will you spend just as much time with your friends, family and work? Why or why not?

_____

_____

_____

_____

11. What type of relationship do you want your spouse to have with your friends?

_____

_____

_____

_____

12. Do you love to have guests in your home for entertainment?

_____

_____

_____

_____

13. Who are your friends? Identify at least three. What is it that makes them your friends?

_____

_____

_____

_____

_____

_____

_____

_____

14. Do you each find yourself continually looking for appropriate ways to make the other happy? Or are you each seeking your own happiness and interests without first considering those of the other?

_____

_____

_____

_____

15. Are you each free to be yourself when you are together, or must you always be on guard?

_____

_____

_____

_____

16. Are there hobbies that he/she engages in that are reckless or too time-consuming? Are you spending less time with him/her because of it?

_____

_____

_____

_____

_____

17. If there is an issue in your relationship that could cause a divorce, what would that issue be? What spiritual ways would he/she use to over come it?

_____

_____

_____

_____

_____

_____

18. One of the most predictive traits for compatibility is if you can sense the other's sadness. Can you tell when he/she is upset?

_____

_____

_____

_____

_____

19. At this stage in your relationship, do you still feel the need to be "on your best behavior," or are you comfortable being yourself?

_____

_____

_____

_____

20. What do you fear in your relationship?

_____

_____

_____

_____

_____

_____

21. If there is one thing you could do but are not currently doing to make your relationship more meaningful, what is it?

_____

_____

_____

_____

22. Do you truly enjoy each other's company? Or do you just enjoy each other when you are doing things you like to do?

_____

_____

_____

_____

23. What do you not like about him or her? (Research tells us you can't change another person, you can only change yourself.) What can you not live with, that he/she does?

_____

_____

_____

_____

_____

_____

_____

24. What do each of you bring to the relationship?

_____

_____

_____

_____

_____

_____

25. Do you uplift one another in public, or do you poke fun at him or her just to get a laugh from your friends?

_____

_____

26. Do you talk positively about him or her to your friends or coworkers? Or, do you dwell mostly on the negative things?

_____

_____

_____

27. Do you agree on music? Is there music that you listen to that is inappropriate? Would you allow your future children to listen to it?

_____

_____

_____

_____

28. Does each of you inspire the other to do his/her best in studies, jobs, Church callings, and other significant responsibilities? Or do you both live below your standards and ideals when you are together?

_____

_____

_____

_____

_____

_____

_____

29. Do you encourage each other's hobbies and talents?

_____

_____

_____

_____

_____

30. If someone were to put you down, would your significant other stand up for you or ignore the situation?

_____

_____

_____

_____

_____

31. Is your significant other overly jealous and possessive? Does he or she need to know exactly where you are at all times of the day? Does he or she call to check up on you?

_____

_____

_____

_____

32. Do you get jealous easily and mistrust for no reason?

_____

_____

_____

33. Is he or she more giving than you? Are you too selfish?

_____

_____

_____

34. As you get older, does your significant other expect or want you to get plastic surgery to improve your looks? How do you feel about that? If you wanted plastic surgery, would he or she be okay with that?

_____

_____

_____

_____

35. Do you think it is okay to divorce someone solely for being diagnosed with depression? What if you had children?

_____

_____

_____

_____

_____

_____

36. Would you be opposed to mental health treatment?

_____

_____

37. If you have male/female friendships and these relationships made your significant other uncomfortable, would you end them for him or her?

_____

_____

_____

38. Do you need to hide who you really are? Or are you confident that you are fully accepted and loved?

_____

_____

_____

_____

39. What are your views on divorce? Did you come from a divorced family? Do you think it is okay to divorce when children are involved? Or would you stay married despite your feelings, for the sake of the children?

_____

_____

_____

_____

_____

40. What type of relationship do you want with your children? Do you expect to be their best friend and give them everything you never got? Or, do you plan to let them experience what "earning a dollar" means?

_____

_____

_____

_____

_____

_____

"If we would know true love and understanding one for another, we must realize that communication is more than a sharing of words. It is the wise sharing of emotions, feelings, and concerns. It is the sharing of oneself totally."

Elder Marvin J. Ashton (1915–94)
of the Quorum of the Twelve Apostles
("Family Communications," *Ensign*, May 1976, 52.)

Past History and
Trust Questions

1. When every couple is married, the partners make vows never to have sexual relations with any other person. How is it that so many people today break these vows? What measures will you take to avoid this happening in your relationship?

_____

_____

_____

_____

_____

_____

_____

_____

_____

2. Is trust automatic until something occurs that takes it away, or does it evolve over time?

_____

_____

_____

_____

3. Are you the type of person that would discuss your private business, whether it is your sex life or relationships, with a best friend other than your current partner? How would you feel if he/she did the same?

_____

_____

_____

_____

_____

_____

_____

4. If you have children from a previous marriage, will your significant other get along with your children? Will he/she be able to handle dealing with an ex-spouse?

_____

_____

_____

_____

5. If your past husband or wife is deceased, are you marrying too soon? (Each person is unique.) Are you comparing your past relationship with the present too much?

_____

_____

_____

6. What is your definition of "flirting"?

_____

_____

_____

_____

7. If one of us cheats, what is the outcome?

_____

_____

_____

8. Is there anything in your past I should be aware of?

_____

_____

_____

_____

9. If your past boyfriends/girlfriends listed your most negative characteristics, what would they be?

_____

_____

_____

_____

_____

_____

10. Have you ever been violent in past relationships?

_____

_____

_____

11. Do you keep letters or pictures from past relationships?

_____

_____

12. Do your friends entice you to see other people? Why?

_____

_____

_____

_____

13. As you were growing up, did you think more about the type of person you wanted to marry, or the type of person you wanted to be for your spouse? Why? Describe your thoughts.

_____

_____

_____

_____

_____

_____

_____

_____

_____

_____

_____

_____

_____

_____

14. Are there any past addictions (gambling, internet pornography, etc.) from your past that your fiancé doesn't know about?

_____

_____

_____

15. Have you ever been able to overcome a bad habit? What was it?

_____

_____

_____

_____

_____

16. Would it concern you if he or she had premarital sex long before he or she met you? What if he or she had that situation resolved by telling the bishop and going through the steps of repentance?

_____

_____

_____

_____

_____

17. Have you ever cheated on a past girlfriend or boyfriend? If so, what is your plan for never doing it again? Why should he or she believe you would never cheat on him or her?

_____

_____

_____

_____

_____

18. Why have you ended relationships in the past?

_____

_____

_____

_____

_____

_____

_____

19. Have you ever been involved in any criminal activity, been in jail or testified for anyone in court?

_____

_____

20. Have you ever had a history of drugs, alcoholism or domestic violence? Is there a history of that in your family? Does he or she control you? Is he or she very jealous?

_____

_____

_____

_____

_____

_____

_____

21. Have you ever seen a psychologist? Been diagnosed with a mental disorder, anxiety or depression? Do you take medicine for a condition? What for, and how much?

_____

_____

_____

_____

22. Has anyone ever had a reason not to trust either of you?

_____

_____

_____

_____

23. What was your childhood like? Was your family an affectionate one?

_____

_____

_____

_____

_____

_____

_____

24. Have you had premarital sex and how often? Have you repented? Is being married in the temple important to you?

_____

_____

_____

_____

_____

_____

_____

25. Is there anyone in your family who is dangerous or sexually abusive?

_____

_____

_____

26. Which childhood or Church experiences influence your behavior and attitudes the most?

_____

_____

_____

_____

_____

27. Could any feelings of affection and romance be revived if you met a previous boyfriend or girlfriend, even though you feel strongly committed to your significant other?

_____

_____

_____

_____

_____

28. How is your relationship different from or similar to the ones you have had in the past?

_____

_____

_____

_____

_____

_____

29. Do you have any health problems he or she should know about?

_____

_____

_____

_____

_____

30. Have you been married before?

_____

_____

_____

31. What would you do if you felt that you had been abused?

_____

_____

_____

_____

_____

_____

32. Whom would you call for assistance, if you were being abused?

_____

_____

_____

_____

33. Are you willing to take a physical exam, before marriage?

_____

_____

_____

34. Is there an embarrassing situation in your life you don't want anyone to know about?

_____

_____

_____

_____

35. Do you have unresolved issues in your life that you need to see the bishop or a psychologist about?

_____

_____

_____

_____

36. If you were previously married, what part of that relationship did you contribute to the divorce? What could you have done differently to make the marriage work?

_____

_____

_____

_____

37. Do you have enemies or anyone in your life that would like to harm you or your future family, either financially or physically?

_____

_____

_____

38. Do you have a violent past or difficulty controlling your anger?

_____

_____

_____

39. Do you think hitting or shoving a person is okay when you're angry?

_____

_____

40. Is there a secret that you are withholding from your friends or family?

_____

_____

_____

41. Does your significant other have a history of any of the following: abusing narcotics or prescription drugs; violence; jealousy; alcoholism; smoking? Do you feel they may still have this problem, or could potentially have this problem in the future?

_____

_____

_____

_____

_____

_____

_____

_____

42. Looking back at your past relationships, what stands out to you as the most common mistake you have made in each of them?

_____

_____

_____

_____

_____

_____

"Your success in marriage will depend largely on your ability to focus on improving yourself, rather than trying to reshape your spouse. It will depend more on being the right one than finding the right one. There is greater power in giving than in getting."

Elder Lynn G. Robbins of the Seventy
("Finding Your Sweetheart," *New Era*, Sept. 2003, 45.)

Character and Self-Worth Questions

1. At what point in a marriage do you feel divorce is appropriate?

_____

_____

_____

_____

_____

_____

2. What is your attitude toward non-members? Are more of your friends non-members than members? Why or why not?

_____

_____

_____

_____

_____

3. Are you possessive about what you currently own? Once you're married will items be equally shared or will they still be "your stuff" and "his/her stuff"?

_____

_____

_____

4. Have you ever found yourself denying something you don't like about him/her, thinking it will go away, or that you are overreacting?

_____

_____

_____

_____

5. Do you feel you should stick with a marriage, even if you're unhappy? Would you stay for the children?

_____

_____

_____

_____

6. Do you feel better about yourself when you are with him or her? Does he or she make you feel like a person of true worth, a child of God?

_____

_____

_____

7. Do you want to associate with someone because of his or her popularity only, or do you look deeper for spiritual and moral qualities?

_____

_____

8. Are you of a different social income than he/she? Are you prepared to adjust to these differences?

_____

_____

_____

_____

9. Why do you attend church? Is it only to socialize, or for deeper spiritual reasons? Or, both?

_____

_____

_____

_____

10. Since mental attitude is important to the success of any venture, what mental attitudes do you hold toward getting married? For example, do you feel pressured into marriage? Are there negative reasons that are motivating an engagement? Boredom, financial freedom, loneliness, insecurity?

_____

_____

_____

_____

11. Since problems seem to take on exaggerated significance when borne in silence, how do you resolve conflict? Do you use prayer to overcome problems?

_____

_____

_____

_____

_____

_____

12. Do you feel too young to get married? Do you feel pressured to get married because everyone else is?

_____

_____

13. How would you describe yourself? How would he/she?

_____

_____

_____

_____

_____

_____

_____

_____

14. Are you a person who cares too much what others think of you? Or are you confident in who you are?

_____

_____

15. How do you handle anger and other emotions?

_____

_____

_____

_____

16. How optimistic are you? How much of your dialogue is negative?

_____

_____

_____

_____

17. In what instances in your life do you feel like a hypocrite?

_____

_____

_____

_____

18. How do you manage adverse events and setbacks? Have you been able to grow through adversity (not just go through it)?

_____

_____

_____

_____

19. What will be different once you get married? Are you expecting to change as a person?

_____

_____

_____

_____

20. What has been your most negative experience with the Church and your most positive? Where does each of you gain your strength when you struggle with your testimony?

_____

_____

_____

_____

_____

21. Do you dress modestly? Will you modify your wardrobe in order to wear garments after being sealed?

_____

_____

22. What is your most negative characteristic? And what are you willing to do to fix it?

_____

_____

_____

_____

_____

_____

_____

23. Do you accept criticism easily?

_____

_____

_____

_____

_____

_____

24. Have you ever thought that you should marry him or her because if you don't, no one else will come along and you will be lonely for the rest of your life?

_____

_____

_____

_____

25. Does having new clothes or nice things give you more self-esteem?

_____

_____

_____

26. Would you be willing to move away from family and friends to follow a career?

_____

_____

_____

27. How would your feelings change about him/her, if he/she gained 10 lbs, 20 lbs or more? What if you gained a lot of weight?

_____

_____

_____

_____

28. What are your political views? Are you a republican, democrat or other? How do you decide whom to vote for? How important is politics to you?

_____

_____

_____

_____

_____

_____

_____

_____

29. Have you ever suppressed your feelings on a particular issue because you were afraid that if you shared them with him or her, he or she wouldn't want to be with you anymore?

_____

_____

_____

30. Why do you feel at this time in your life you are ready to get married?

_____

_____

_____

_____

31. Are there things that you have not accomplished that you want to do before you get married?

_____

_____

_____

_____

_____

32. What can you offer your mate, spiritually?

_____

_____

_____

_____

_____

_____

33. What do you read? Is it uplifting?

_____

_____

_____

_____

_____

34. How do you express your feelings and gratitude to someone who has done a favor for you?

_____

_____

_____

_____

35. How much time passes before you choose to forgive someone?

_____

_____

_____

36. Do you believe that we choose our own course in life, or it is preor-dained?

_____

_____

_____

37. Are you overly choosy in a mate? Are you trying to seek perfection but can't find it?

_____

_____

_____

_____

_____

"May I say that almost all marriages could be beautiful, harmonious, happy, and eternal ones, if the two people primarily involved would determine that it should be, that it must be, that it will be."

President Spencer W. Kimball

("Marriage Is Honorable," Speeches of the Year,
Provo: Brigham Young University Press, 1973, 257.)

Love, Intimacy, and Communication Questions

1. What are your views on being physically abused? Would you leave your marriage after the first incident of abuse?

_____

_____

_____

_____

_____

_____

_____

_____

2. What are your views on fidelity? How many affairs would it take for you to decide to divorce?

_____

_____

_____

_____

_____

3. Do you support one another when it comes to diet, homework, and career choices?

_____

_____

_____

4. What does "commitment" mean to you?

_____

_____

_____

_____

_____

_____

_____

_____

5. Does either of you want to date anyone else? Are you prepared to leave the dating scene behind and enter a monogamous relationship? Sometimes that means giving up a lifestyle of hanging out with single friends. Are you prepared to make the changes?

_____

_____

_____

_____

6. Do you have any problems with intimacy in the confines of a married relationship? Do you have sexual expectations when you're married that are unrealistic?

_____

_____

_____

_____

7. If you were to eliminate your physical attraction for each other, what would be left?

_____

_____

_____

_____

_____

8. Have you ever had a fight with him/her? How often? What about?

_____

_____

_____

_____

_____

_____

_____

9. Have you ever felt that he/she takes you for granted? When?

_____

_____

_____

_____

_____

_____

_____

_____

_____

10. Do you love this person? Define love. What is your concept of marriage?

_____

_____

_____

_____

_____

_____

_____

_____

_____

_____

11. How do you show love to each other? Does he or she have emotional self-awareness? How are they at empathy?

_____

_____

_____

_____

_____

12. How does he try to make you feel loved and validated? Does it work? How do you try to make him feel loved and validated? Does it work?

_____

_____

_____

_____

_____

13. Are there any questions that you feel uncomfortable asking him or her? Any topics that you feel uncomfortable being asked?

_____

_____

_____

_____

_____

14. Is there anything about marriage that frightens you?

_____

_____

_____

_____

_____

15. What is the best way for me to communicate difficult feelings about you so that you are not offended?

_____

_____

_____

_____

_____

16. Who should know about the arguments we have?

_____

_____

_____

_____

17. Do you feel you could communicate with me under any circumstance and about any subject?

_____

_____

_____

_____

_____

_____

_____

_____

18. Do you love and respect him or her enough that you give careful consideration to his or her ideas and feelings, and make all possible decisions together? Are you willing to follow his or her ideas when they seem more inspired and correct than your own?

_____

_____

_____

_____

_____

19. What attitudes will grieve the Spirit and cause it to be withdrawn from your home?

_____

_____

_____

_____

_____

20. Do you fight now? If so, how often?

_____

_____

_____

_____

_____

_____

_____

21. If you find it hard to admit you're wrong about something, what can you do to overcome this reluctance?

_____

_____

_____

_____

_____

_____

22. Can you afford the wedding he or she wants?

_____

_____

_____

_____

23. Is there anyone who feels you shouldn't get married? Do they have a valid reason?

_____

_____

_____

_____

24. Do you feel comfortable meeting with the bishop for premarital counseling?

_____

_____

_____

25. Describe your dream marriage and dream wedding. Is any of this realistic?

_____

_____

_____

_____

_____

_____

_____

_____

_____

_____

26. If there is one issue that would cause you to divorce, what is it? How will we ensure that it doesn't lead to a divorce?

_____

_____

_____

_____

_____

_____

_____

_____

27. Are you allergic to pets?

_____

28. Can you live with the pet he or she currently owns?

_____

29. Why have you chosen him or her for your potential spouse?

_____

_____

_____

_____

_____

_____

_____

_____

_____

30. How do you expect your spouse to express anger?

_____

_____

_____

_____

_____

31. When do you think it is appropriate to initiate mediation in a marriage? Would you be willing to meet with the Bishop or a marriage counselor?

_____

_____

_____

_____

_____

32. When there is a dispute in your marriage, religious or not, how should the conflict get resolved?

_____

_____

_____

_____

_____

33. Define mental, verbal, emotional, and physical abuse.

_____

_____

_____

_____

_____

_____

_____

_____

34. How long should an engagement last?

_____

_____

35. How old should a person be before he or she gets married?

_____

_____

36. If you marry before you turn 25 years old, list what life experiences you feel you may miss because of your decision to marry early.

_____

_____

_____

_____

_____

37. How long should you wait before telling your family about your engagement?

_____

_____

38. Who should you tell first about your engagement?

_____

_____

39. Do you still rely on your parents for financial help or advice? Will this continue after your married? Are you dependent on your parents or are you ready to accept your own choices and responsibilities in life?

_____

_____

_____

40. What do you fear about being or getting married?

_____

_____

_____

_____

41. Do you have any racial prejudices? What if your daughter or son wanted to date outside his or her race?

_____

_____

_____

_____

_____

_____

42. In what ways will you communicate love to your spouse on a daily basis? Do you feel it is necessary to say "I love you" daily? Do you do that now? Why or why not?

_____

_____

_____

_____

_____

_____

"[Divine love] is not like that association of the world which is misnamed love, but which is mostly physical attraction. … The love of which the Lord speaks is not only physical attraction, but also faith, confidence, understanding, and partnership. It is devotion and companionship, parenthood, common ideals and standards. It is cleanliness of life and sacrifice and unselfishness. This kind of love never tires nor wanes. It lives on through sickness and sorrow, through prosperity and privation, through accomplishment and disappointment, through time and eternity."

President Spencer W. Kimball
(*The Teachings of Spencer W. Kimball*, 1982, 248.)

Social Media
and Technology
Questions

1. Does it matter to you or not if I remain friends with an ex on my Facebook page?

_____

_____

2. If I didn't like someone on your Facebook or Twitter account would you remove them?

_____

_____

3. Are our social media sites our privacy or should we be on all of them?

_____

_____

_____

4. Do we have trust on social media sites? Is he or she posting their status as "in a relationship"? Are there pictures of one another together?

_____

_____

_____

_____

5. Will we limit the time we spend on our cell phones and social media sites when we are together?

_____

_____

_____

6. Do you think it is okay for our future children to have cell phones or social media accounts?

_____

_____

7. Do you think it is rude to answer text messages or emails while we are spending time with one another?

_____

_____

_____

8. Will we have a joint Facebook page?

_____

_____

9. Do you think it is safe for us to post pictures of our kids online or should we keep that private?

_____

_____

_____

10. Do you agree to us installing parental controls that block certain websites on our computer?

_____

_____

11. Do I have the right to read your emails or texts when ever I want to?

_____

_____

12. Do you believe that we have the right to read our children's text messages or emails without their consent?

_____

_____

13. Do you have any addictions to online porn or online games?

_____

_____

14. How much time do you think our kids should be allowed to play video games?

_____

_____

15. Will we access to each others passwords, computers and cell phones or are some things private to each other in our relationship?

_____

_____

16. Is his or her behavior acceptable online? Is it different?

_____

_____

_____

_____

17. Will we do online banking or the old fashioned way?

_____

_____

18. Are there any friends you don't want on my social media sites?

_____

_____

_____

_____

About the Author

Shannon L. Alder is an inspirational author that writes on the topic of relationships. Her tidbits of wisdom have been published in over 100 different books, by various relationship authors, and in several online magazine articles (*Psychology Today*, *Huffington Post*, etc.). She runs an online Facebook community dedicated to staying positive. You can become a part of her tribe of misfits by visiting www.facebook.com/StayingPositiveUniversity. All the proceeds of her books go toward sending her on medical missions around the world. In addition to her humanitarian work, she owns The Positivity Shop™ an online store that sells fair trade goods and eco-friendly products. Plus, products that support various global and social causes. Visit StayingPositiveUniversity.com.

Scan to visit

StayingPositiveUniversity.com